WIND HORSE INDIANS

by Ron Edward Cyscon

Library of Congress Number: 2005906674
ISBN: Softcover   978-1-5992-6212-3
            Hardcover   978-1-5992-6215-4

Print information available on the last page

Rev. date: 01/25/2019

To order additional copies of this book, contact:
Xlibris
1-888-795-4274
www.Xlibris.com
Orders@Xlibris.com

ALL MY LOVE AND THANKS TO
MY BUSHA, MY MOM, TIFFANY AND KASHA
FOR BELIEVING IN ME –

RON -

THANKS TO MOLLY AND DUANE
FOR THE FANTASTIC ARTWORK -

ONCE UPON A TIME IN AMERICA, WHEN IT WAS VERY YOUNG. THERE WAS A TRIBE OF INDIANS CALLED "THE WIND HORSE INDIANS". THEY WERE CALLED THAT BECAUSE THEY WOULD RAISE HORSES THAT COULD RUN LIKE THE WIND!

SOME PEOPLE EVEN SAID IF THEY HAD WINGS THEY COULD FLY!
   PEOPLE FROM ALL OVER WOULD COME TO THE WIND HORSE INDIANS, FOR BEAUTIFUL FAST HORSES.

DUANE GILLOGLY

AS TIME WENT ON, MORE PEOPLE STARTED TO LIVE IN AMERICA. PEOPLE MADE LOG CABINS, SOME MADE FARMS, OTHERS MADE BIG RANCHES. SO THE MORE PEOPLE AND MORE FAMILIES THAT MOVED IN MADE IT VERY HARD FOR THE WIND HORSE INDIANS TO RAISE THEIR WONDERFUL HORSES.

TIMES HAD PASSED AND THERE WAS NOT SUCH A NEED FOR STRONG BEAUTIFUL, FAST HORSES ANYMORE. THE LAND WHERE THE WIND HORSE INDIANS RAISED THEIR HORSES HAD BECOME VERY CROWDED. SOME PEOPLE EVEN STARTED TO COMPLAIN!

MORE TIME WENT BY, AND A GROUP OF PEOPLE GOT TOGETHER AND WENT TO THE WIND HORSE INDIAN'S CHIEF AND TOLD HIM THAT THEY NEED HIS LAND, FOR MORE LOG CABINS, FARMS, AND RANCHES.

DUANE GILLOGLY

THE CHIEF WAS VERY HURT! HE TOLD THE PEOPLE THAT THE LAND BELONGED TO THE WIND HORSE INDIANS; BUT THEY DID NOT WANT TO LISTEN. ALL THEY WANTED WAS HIS LAND. THEY GAVE THE CHIEF THREE DAYS TO MOVE AWAY.

ON THE FIRST DAY THE CHIEF CALLED A POW-WOW OF ALL THE
WIND HORSE INDIANS, AND TOLD THEM WHAT HAD HAPPENED!

ALL THE INDIAN MEN, WOMEN, AND CHILDREN WERE VERY UPSET. THEY DID NOT KNOW WHAT TO DO. THE INDIAN CHIEF WAS OLD, BUT VERY WISE, HE KNEW THIS WAS COMING AND HE HAD ALREADY TAKEN PRECAUTION!

DUANE GILLOGLY

13

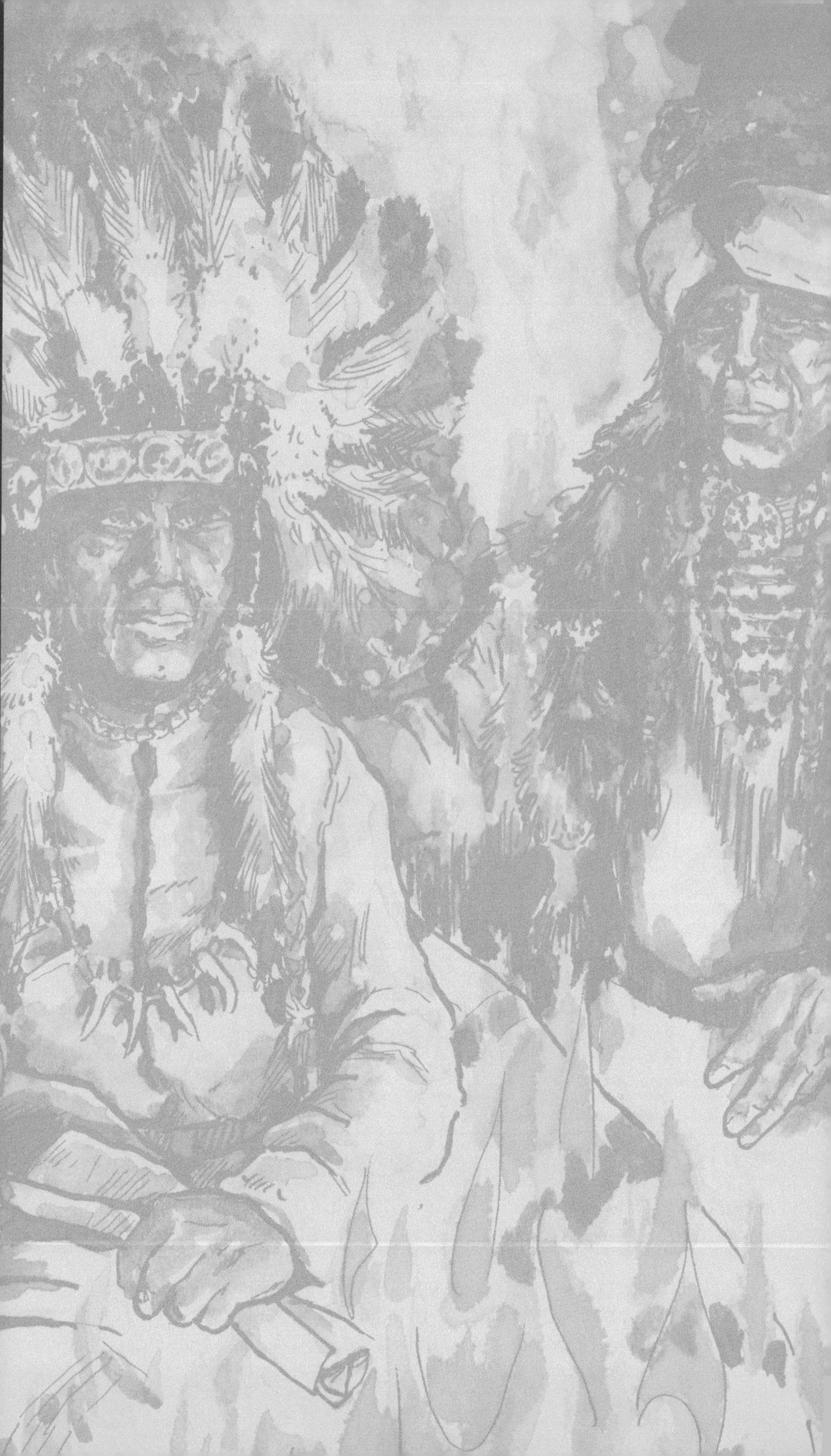

ON THE SECOND DAY THE CHIEF CALLED HIS MEDICINE MAN AND ASKED HIM IF HE WAS READY AND IF HE COULD PERFORM THE SPECIAL MAGIC NECESSARY TO SAVE THE WIND HORSE INDIANS! THE MEDICINE MAN SAID YES!

DUANE GILLOGLY 15

ON THE THIRD DAY THE CHIEF HAD THE INDIANS GET ALL THE HORSES AND LINE THEM UP, HE HAD ALL THE INDIANS PICK THEIR FAVORITE HORSE AND TOLD THEM "GET READY TO RIDE!"

WITH THAT THE MEDICINE MAN MADE A FIRE, GOT HIS FAVORITE HORSE AND STARTED TO RIDE AROUND THE FIRE FASTER AND FASTER, SINGING A SPECIAL INDIAN PRAYER, RIDING FASTER AND FASTER, SINGING LOUDER AND LOUDER. WITH A SNAP OF YOUR FINGER IT WAS DONE .....THE WIND HORSE INDIANS WERE IN THEIR NEW HOME!

LATER ON THAT THIRD DAY, THE GROUP OF PEOPLE THAT TOLD THE WIND HORSE INDIANS TO GO, WENT TO WHERE THE INDIANS USED TO LIVE. TO THEIR AMAZEMENT NOTHING COULD BE FOUND, NOT ONE HORSE, NOT ONE MAN, WOMAN OR CHILD. EVEN THE TEE-PEE'S WERE GONE!!!

OH THERE WAS ONE THING THE PEOPLE FOUND AFTER RIDING AROUND FOR HOURS AND THAT WAS THEIR TOTEM POLE; AND GUESS WHAT WAS AT THE TOP? THE MOST BEAUTIFUL AND WONDERFUL WIND HORSE WITH WINGS!!!

DUANE GILLOGLY

FOR YOUR ENJOYMENT PLEASE CONNECT DOTS NUMBERED 1 - 97 TO SEE WHAT'S IN THE CLOUDS.

NOT MANY PEOPLE PAID MUCH ATTENTION TO IT, NOT MANY PEOPLE UNDERSTOOD IT, BUT TO THIS VERY DAY IF YOU LOOK UP AT THE CLOUDS YOU JUST MIGHT SEE A WIND HORSE, THE CHIEF OR A TEE-PEE. ON A WINDY DAY, YOU'LL NEVER KNOW IF A WIND HORSE WAS OUT FOR A RUN OR IN THE EVENING WHAT SOME PEOPLE CALL A FALLING STAR COULD BE A WIND HORSE, JUST LIKE THE ONE ON THE TOP OF THE TOTEM POLE; OUT FOR A NITE-TIME RIDE.

Duane   Gillogly

21

Printed in the United States
By Bookmasters